The Great Domesday Book Of Ipswich, Liber Sextus: With An Introduction To The Entire Volume

Richard Percyvale

In the interest of creating a more extensive selection of rare historical book reprints, we have chosen to reproduce this title even though it may possibly have occasional imperfections such as missing and blurred pages, missing text, poor pictures, markings, dark backgrounds and other reproduction issues beyond our control. Because this work is culturally important, we have made it available as a part of our commitment to protecting, preserving and promoting the world's literature. Thank you for your understanding.

THE GREAT DOMESDAY BOOK OF IPSWICH,

COMPILED BY RICHARD PERCYVALE.

12 HENRY VIII.

LIBER SEXTUS.

WITH AN INTRODUCTION TO THE ENTIRE VOLUME AND THE EARLIER
DOMESDAY BOOKS BELONGING TO THE TOWN.

The ancient Borough of Ipswich, besides possessing a rather remarkable and extensive collection of Rolls, Charters and Letters Patent, Deeds, both private and municipal, as well as other miscellaneous writings of varied worth, is fortunate in having among the town Archives, several books, both written and printed, which are of special value and importance, alike to the antiquary and historian, and of no small account in the eyes of the intelligent burgess, who rightly regards each as a link in the silver chain that connects the present with the past. The interest which attaches to these volumes may be said mainly to centre in those, known respectively as the 'New' or 'Great' Domesday and the 'Old' or 'Little' Domesday Book, concerning which, and especially the former, I desire to draw attention.

The ancient laws and customs of Ipswich, dating from a very early period of the town's constitution and history, were originally contained in certain Rolls, once the cherished inheritance of our forefathers, but which, alas! were in the 56th year of the reign of Henry III.

abstracted from the "Comyn Hutche or Cheste" and, regardless of the grievous injury inflicted thereby upon the town, purloined by a certain notorious Town Clerk *("un faus comun Clerk")* one, John le Blake, of whom, and the precious Rolls, it is almost needless to say, nothing further was heard. 'Men of the East' are proverbially '*wise*,' so that it is no cause for surprise, that we find the Ipswich townsfolk soon after this occurence, deputing to twenty-four of their number, the task of compiling afresh an account of the ancient usages of the Borough, of the extreme importance of which they thus appear to have been fully sensible. These revived customs, ordinances and regulations, were embodied in the volume since known as the "*Domesday des Leyes e des usages de Gippeswiz,*" but more commonly as the 'Little Domesday Book,' and appears to have been completed in the 19th year of Edward I. This work, however, seems very soon after to have disappeared, but not before two official copies had been made sometime during the reign of Edward II., and these were a little later on, increased to the number of three.

Of the fourteenth century transcripts, one is an octavo volume, containing within its leather covers, ninety-one leaves of vellum, upon fifty of which, appear in a neat hand, a copy in French of the former Domesday Book, while sundry other matters, of a later period, occupy the remaining forty one skins.

The other transcript, or duplicate copy, is apparently the work of the same penman, and also contains on the leaves not used for the original purpose of the book, much interesting matter of a subsequent date.

A third transcript of a similar character, and executed probably *about* the same time as the two copies just mentioned, but every way inferior to them, found its way some twenty-five years ago into the hands of the British Museum authorities,[*] under circumstances

---

[*] "Le Domesday des Leyes et Usages de Gippewiz 19 Edw: I. *Br: Mus:* CLVII. B. *Add* MSS. 25,011.

detailed at length in the Report recently made by Mr. J. C. Jeaffreson for the Historical MSS. Commission (Appendix ix, p. 242). Beside the French text, this copy has an English translation, and is easily accessible to the student in an admirable edition published in the Roll series,* which has an able introduction, pointing out especially the importance of the Ipswich Domesday as a unique volume among a rare class of documents: valuable foot notes, explanatory of obsolete terms, &c., are to be found on nearly every page.

In addition to this volume, a fifteenth century copy of this Domesday, was, at the same time as the other transcript mentioned, purchased by the Trustees of the British Museum, in whose custody it remains.

This latter volume was in all probability the precursor of the 'new' or 'Great' Domesday Book, so called from having been compiled in the 12th year of Henry VIII, and owing also to its great size, compared with the earlier transcripts of the former Domesday. Except only in point of priority of date, the Great Domesday Book of Richard Percyvale, (formerly one of the Portmen of the Town,) is a volume of far greater interest and importance than the earlier volumes to which allusion has been made, and supplied, what must have been a long felt want, in giving (to use the words of the compiler) "*as many of the old grants, liberties, ordinances, laws and good constitutions,*" as he could find "*prescription or good matter of record for, with divers and sundry other matters right necessary to be had and known in the town and borough of Ipswich.*" (see Prologue.)

The Great Domesday Book is a finely written thick folio, bound in old embossed calf, measuring 16 in. by 12 in. and containing 271 leaves of vellum, the whole being divided into seven Books (preceded by the prologue) which are as follows:—

LIBER PRIMUS, contains the Charter granted in the first year of the reign of King John, followed by records

---

* The Black Book of the Admiralty, Appendix, Part ii, vol. ii, 1873. Edited by Sir Travers Twiss, Q.C., D.C.L.

of succeeding grants, &c., as far as 13 Edward I. This book is mainly taken up with matter contained in the Little Domesday Volume and consists of twenty-one vellum leaves, and one leaf blank. (It is preceded by five blank leaves, upon the back of one of these a memorandum is written.)

LIBER SECUNDUS, has an English rendering of the eighty-three chapters contained in the earlier volume, where it is given in French; to these ordinances and regulations affecting the municipal life, twenty others of a latter date are added in Latin, the most remarkable being those for the proper ordering of the religious observances connected with the famous Merchants Guild of Corpus Christi. This book occupies no less than fifty-eight leaves: there are beside seventeen that are plain.

LIBER TERTIUS, is taken up with

(1) An Ordinance for the regulation of the *beremen* or *Wynedraggers* (porters) as laid down in the Little Domesday.

(2) The Toune Custumes belonging to the Kynge's fee-ferme.

(3) The Assise of weying of brede after the Statue of Wynchester.

(4) The Assyse for bruers.

This book contains fifteen leaves, with one left plain at the end.

LIBER QUARTUS, has in Latin "the constitucion for Corpus Christi procession and in what maner the Maundy shulde yerely be kepte with other dyuers remembraunces requesyte to be had in memory;" followed by an order "how euery occupacion or craftesmen shuld ordre themselffes in their goyng * * * in the same procession." There are also between 30 and 40 other distinct entries consisting of copies of Indentures, acquittances, enrolments, grants, extracts, memorandums, &c., &c., the whole occupying seventy-eight leaves, 18 or 19 of which are written in a late (bad) hand (*temp.* Eliz: and Ph: and

Mary) and two blank leaves. Three leaves that follow, which may also be said to form part of Book iv, contain in several different hands, various oaths added at a subsequent time to those which appear in Book v. so as to meet the requirements of after legislation, viz.

(*a*) The Bailiffs (as to Impanelling Juries.)
(*b*) Justices of the Peace.
(*c*) Searchers of Leather.
(*d*) Sealer of Leather.
(*e*) Fleshwardens.
(*f*) Wardens of the Foundation (29 *Sep.* 1623)
(*g*) Town Treasurer.
(*h*) Clavigers.

The fourth book is thus by far the largest portion of the several divisions marked in the volume, and has the widest range of subjects.

LIBER QUINTUS, is by reason of its contents, that part of the book which in former days was most frequently called into requisition, and from it, the markets &c., were periodically proclaimed. It consists of twenty leaves, which bear marks of long continued usage, at the end of which are two blank leaves, and contains "alle the othes that euery bayliff, portman, burgeys and alle other officers be wonte to swere when they be admyttyd into ther romys and offices with other dyuerse articules that the bayliffes of this towne be bounde to se obserued and kepte and to proclayme them euery yere in dyuers places of this Town with the Libertyes of this town by water and by land."

LIBER SEXTUS, may claim to be regarded as a book possessing more general interest than the others. The greater part of the contents of this portion, is taken up with matters relating, not to Ipswich only, but to the whole County of Suffolk *i.e.* (1) Taxes paid by every town in Suffolk to the King's Grace. (2) List of Knights' Fees of the Honors of Lancaster and Leicester in the County of Suffolk. It contains also, (*a*) a curious heraldic description of the arms borne by divers Sovereigns; (*b*) a quaint memorandum of ancient lineal measurements, and what I have elsewere spoken of as, (*c*) a "Rhyming Chronicle of the Kings of England," (William I. to Edward IV.), and attributed to Lydgate, the Monk-poet of Bury,* which brings the sixth book to a conclusion. There are in this part, twenty leaves, three of which remain blank.

LIBER SEPTIMUS, is the last book: it contains the Charter confirmed to the town in the 3rd year of Henry VIII. with another Charter relating to the Admiralty, and sundry other matters, written upon nineteen leaves, and there are beside, nine leaves at the end left plain.

The character and contents of the Great Doomsday Book, as well as the object and design of its predecessors, may, it is thought from this description, be deemed of sufficient interest to lead many to desire a further and fuller acquaintance with the volume, such as a study of the book in its entirety can alone give.

It will be seen that the Great Domesday Book, is in point of fact, what in process of time the earlier Domesday volumes were inclined to become, a veritable *olla podrida*, for, if not exactly a receptacle for "odds and ends," many of the entries there made, cannot but be regarded as altogether foreign to the original purpose for which such a book was designed. We have, however, abundant cause for satisfaction, that the Great Domesday Book, is in respect of its varied contents, just what it is; the antiquary especially will be sure to find pleasure in the preservation of such quaint things as some which are here recorded, and which might otherwise have disappeared altogether. This feature is prominent in, and indeed may be said in a great measure to be confined to, the sixth book. Beside all this the inhabitant of Suffolk may find therein matters of some importance to the whole County, which perhaps point to a position, more or less one of pre-eminence, which may have been

* East Anglian, *New Ser.*, vol. I., pp. 38, 41.

occupied by the town of Ipswich in the reign of Henry VI. and have caused the Borough to be regarded also as a 'remembrancer' and custodian for the County at large. The section which best illustrates this conjecture, is the following account, also from the sixth book, of the "*taxes paid by every Town in Suffolk to the King's Grace,*" which deserves to be made accessible to all who are interested in the history of the County. Of such taxes it may be said, that originally the amount payable to the King was uncertain, being levied by fresh assessments at each grant made by the Commons, but in the 8th year of Edward III. new taxations were made, by virtue of the King's Commission, of every township &c. in the kingdom, which quite settled the tax payable in each several case, and for the County of Suffolk, is that here recorded.

Richard Percybale's Great Domesday Book. 12 Henry biii.
Liber Sextus.

"HERE BEGYNNETH THE VIth PARTE OF THIS BOKE AND FIRST FOLOWITH WHAT TAXES EV̄Y TOWÑ IN SUFFOLK PAYETH TO THE KYNGS GRACE.

Villa de Gip̄p̄o cū hamleta de Wyks Ufford hamleta de Wykys Episcopi hamleta de Stoke et hamleta de Brokys halle LXIIIj*li* x*s* v*d*
Et Inde p donat₁ in Anno xxxij° Rege henrici sexti p dictā dmn̄
Regem ———————————— xx*li*
    Et sic Remān ———XLIIIj*li* x*s* v*d.*
Unde hamleta de Wyks Ufford soluit ——— xxvj*s* viii*d.*
Item hamleta de Wyks epī soluit ——— xxiiij*s*
Item hamleta de Stoke soluit ——— xv*s*
Item hamleta de Brokys soluit ——— vIIj*s*
Item Burgus Gip̄p̄i soluit resid viz ——— xL*li* xvj*s* ix*d*
Burgus dunwici soluit ——— xij*li*
Burgus de Orford soluit ——— x*li*
Burgus de Eye soluit ——— vII*li*   xx*d.*
Sm̄ Burgoꝝ β dict cū hamlets–IIIj^x ——— xII*li* xx*s* ij*d*

The hundred of Samford.

Kyrketoñ alias Shotley	iijli	vjs	ijd.
Unde p donatur p dicts Regem		xvs	
ffreston		xxjs	iiijd
Unde p donatur p dicts Regē		ixs	
Stratfford		xlvijs	iiijd
Unde p donatr p dicts Regem		xijs.	
Berhōlt	vli		
Unde p donatur p dict Regem		vijs	viiid
Horkysted		xxxijs	viiid
Unde p donatur p dicts Regem		vjs	viiid
Capell soluit	iijli	vs	
Unde p donatur p dicts Regem		xxvjs	viiid
Tatyngston soluit		xxxs	ivd
Unde p donatur p dict Regem		xs	
Whersted soluit		xxxjs	ob
Unde p donatur p dicts Regem		viijs	
Copdok soluit		xljs	vjd
Unde p donatur p dicts Regem		xijs	iiijd.
Wenham Magna & pua sol		ls	vjd
Unde p donatur p dicts Regem		xxxs	
Holton soluit		xxxvijs.	vid.
Unde p donatur p dicts Regem		xs.	
Bentley soluit		xls.	
Unde p donatur p dicts Regem		vjs.	
Holbroke soluit		xljs.	xd.
Unde p donatur p dicts Regem		viijs.	
Sprowtoñ soluit	iiijli	xiijs.	
Unde p donatur p dicts Regem		xs.	
Hegham soluit		xxxvijs.	vjd.
Unde p donatur p dicts Regē		vijs.	vjd.
Hynlyshm̄ soluit		liijs.	ijd ob
Unde p donatur p dicts Regē.		xs.	
Burstall soluit		xxvs.	vijq
Unde p donatur p dicts Regem		vjs.	
Shelley soluit		xlvijs	viijd
Unde p donatur p dictū Regem		xijs.	
Reydon soluit	iiijli	vijs	ijd.
Unde p donatur p dictū Regem		xviijs.	
Branthm̄ soluit		lvjs.	
Unde p donatur p dictū Regem		xijs	iiijd.
Belstead pua soluit		xxxvjs	iiid.
Unde p donatur p dictu Regē		xs.	
Stuttoñ soluit		xls	vid.
Unde p donatur p dictū Regē		xs.	
Eūwardeñ soluit		xliiijs	viijd
Unde p donatur p dictū Regē		xs.	

Belsted Magna soluit		Lvj*s*	vi*d*.
Unde p donatur p dictū Regē		x*s*.	
Chelmyngtoū & Wolūston taxantur ad decuman	} iij*li*		
Unde p donatur p dictu Regem		xvj*s*.	
Bona mobilia hered Willi de Berham in villa de Berhm̄ & Capell	}	xiij*s*	iiij*d*
Sm̄ hundred p' dcī cū bona mobilia hered Willi de Barhm̄—Lxj*li* viij v*d*. p̃ Inde £	iij*li*		
Sm̄ total—Lxj*li* vs q̢ Alloc	xviij*li*	viij	ij*d*.
Sm̄ de Claro	xLij*li*	xvj*s*.	x*d* q̢

Hundrę de Bosmerę

Berkyng cū Nedehm̄ sol	v*li*	xvj*s*.	iiij*d*.
Eston cū Wyllershm sol	iij*li*	x*s*.	
Somershm̄ cū fflokton sol	iij*li*		
Unde p donatur p dictū Regē		xx*s*.	
Blakenhm̄ pua soluit		xxxviij*s*.	vi*d*.
Unde p donatur p dictū Regem		xIij*s*.	iiij*d*.
Hemyngstoū soluit		xLvj*s*.	vj*d*.
Unde p donatur p dictū Regem		xIIj*s*.	iiij*d*.
Beylhm̄ soluit		Liij*s*.	x*d*.
Unde p donatur p dictū Regem		xxij*s*.	
Blakenhm̄ magna soluit		xxxiij*s*.	vj*d*.
Netylsted soluit		xxviij*s*.	vi*d*.
Unde p donatur p dictū Regem		xx*s*.	
Ryngesheld soluit	iiij*li*	iiij*s*.	vj*d*.
Unde p donatur p dictū Regem		xxvj*s*.	viij*d*.
Ayshe soluit		xLiiij*s*.	
Estoū Gosbak sol		xxx*s*.	xj*d*.
Unde p donatur p dictū Regem		xv*s*.	
Stonhm̄ Antegan cū mekelfeld sol	iiij*li*	xIII*s*.	x*d*.
Unde p donatur p dictu Regem		xvij*s*	viiij*d*
Stonhm̄ Jernegan soluit		xLvj*s*.	
Stonhm̄ Comitis soluit		Lix*s*.	vij*d*
Unde p donatur p dict Regem		xx*s*.	
Cretyng Sā Olavi Scē Marie et Ōmi Sco% sol	iiij*li*		vj*d*.
Batysford cū Badke sol	iiij*li*		xx*d*.
Unde p donatur p dicts Regem		xx*s*	
Codynhm̄ cum Croeffeld sol	v*li*	xiiij*s*	viij*d*
Unde p donatur p dicts Regem		xx*s*	
Bramfford cum Burstall sol	vj*li*	xvij*s*	viii*d*.
Unde p donatur p dictum Regem		xx*s*.	
Brysete magna & pua		L*s*	ij*d*.
Sm̄ hundr β̃ dicts	Lxiij*li*	IX*s*	iij*d*.

hundr⁴ de hertysmere.

Mendylesham soluit	vj*li*		ij*d*
Unde p donatur p dictū Regem		viijs.	
Redgraue soluit	v*li*	xijs.	iiij*d*.
Unde p donatur p dictum Regem		xxs.	
Palgrave soluit		xLs	ix*d*
Unde p donatur p dictū Regem		viijs.	
Broome		xLjs	ij*d*.
Unde p donatur p dict⁹ Regem		xs	
Westethorp	iij*li*		
Unde p donatur p dict⁹ Regem		xs	
Rysehangyll		xxxvs	iiij*d*
Unde p donatur p dict⁹ Regem		viijs	
Ocle	iij*li*		x*d*.
Unde p donatur p dict⁹ doᵐ Regē		xs.	
Cranele Cokelynge langtoñ ⁊ Suddon } Ad. xᵐ	x*li*	xxs.	vj*d*.
Gyslynghm̄	iij*li*	xiijs.	ix*d* ob
Unde p donatur p dict⁹ Regē		xs.	
Stutton		xxxvijs	
Breseworth		xxxijs.	ij*d*.
Unde p donatur p dict⁹ Regem		vijs.	
Redelyngfeld		xxvij	vij*d* ob
Unde p donatur p dict⁹ Regē		xvjs.	
Thakesle		Lijs	iij*d*.
Unde p donatur p dict⁹ doᵐ Rege		viijs.	
Rekynghale pua		xxxviijs.	viij*d*.
Unde p donatur p dict⁹ Regem		xs.	
Thardoñ taxatur ad xᵃᵐ	iiij*li*	iiijs.	iiij*d*.
Unde p donatʳ p dict⁹ Regem		xs.	
Wyeham		Liiijs.	
Unde p donatʳ p dict⁹ Regem		vjs.	
Baketon	iij*li*	ijs.	viij*d*.
Unde p donatur p dict⁹ Regē		viijs.	
Tharueston	iij*li*	xiiijs.	iiij*d*.
Wortham	v*li*	xs	vj*d*
Unde p donatur p dict⁹ doᵐ Regem		xijs.	
Burgate		Lvs	x*d*.
Unde p donatur p doᵐ Regem antedict'		xs.	
Thornham pua		xviijs.	
Unde p donatur p dict⁹ Regem			viij*d*.
Aspale		xLjs	
Unde p donatur p dict⁹ Regem		vjs.	
Ocolt cū Benynghm̄ taxatˣ ad xᵐ		Liijs	iij*d*
			Ite ij*d*
Unde p donatʳ p dict⁹ Regem		xvjs	
Stoke		xLvjs	viij*d*.

Wyßston ———————————————		xLIIs	IIjd.
Unde p donatur p dictʒ Regem ————		vjs.	
Melles ———————————————		xLVs	vId
Unde p donatur p dictʒ doᵐ Regem ———		vs	vId.
ffenynghm̄ ———————————————	IIjli	xvIjs.	
Unde p donatur p dictʒ Regem ————		xIjs.	
Wederyngsete cū Brokford —————	iiijli	xs	xd.
Unde p donatur p dictʒ Regem ————		xijs.	
Cotton———————————————	iijli	xs.	
Unde p donatur p dictʒ Regem ————		viijs.	
Thornham magna —————————		LVIIIs.	Ijd.
Thweyte ———————————————		xxxs.	
Unde p donatur p dict Regē————		xIIjs	IIIjd.
Sm̄ hundrᵈ β̄ dcē IIIjˣˣ ——————	xIjli	vjs	vIjd.
Inde xᵈ.	xIjli	xiijs.	Id.

hundrdʒ de Cleydoft.

helmynghm̄ ———————————————	IIjli	Ixs	vIIjd	oƀ
Unde p donatur p dictʒ Regē ————		xvjs.		
Cleydon ———————————————		xLiijs	xd.	
Unde p donatur p dictʒ Rege ————		xs.		
Akenhm̄ ———————————————		xxxiiijs	vjd.	
Unde p donatʳ p dictʒ Regem ————		xxs.		
Thurleston cū Whytton —————		Liijs.	vjd.	
Unde p donatur p dictʒ Rege————		xxs.		
Berenghum̄ ———————————————		xxxiiijs	vjd.	
Unde p donatʳ p dictʒ Rege ————		vjs.		
Westerfeld cū Swynlond —————		xLVIjs	vjd.	
Unde p donatur p dictʒ Rege ————		xiijs	iiijd.	
henley ———————————————		xLVs	vjd.	
Unde p donatur p dictʒ Rege————		xxs.		

Sm̄ hundred de Stowe.

Weste Cretyng ———————————————		xLVs.		
Unde p donatur p dictʒ doᵐ Rege ———		xs		
Wetherden ———————————————	IIjli	vjs	xjd	
Unde p donatur p dictʒ doᵐ Rege ———		xiijs	iiijd.	
Gyppyng cū Newton —————		xxxs.		
Unde p donatur p dictʒ Rege ————		xs.		
Onhows cū herlston & Shelond ———		Liijs.		
Unde p donatur p dictʒ Regem ————		viijs.		
ffynbregh magna —————————		liijs.	iiijd.	
Unde p donatur p dictʒ Regem ————		vjs.	vIIjd.	
Buxale ———————————————	iijli	iiijs	IIIjd.	
dagworth———————————————		xxvs.		
Newton Veta ———————————		xLjs	iijd.	
Combes cū ffynbregh pua —————	vjli	xs	vjd	oƀ q.

Unde p donatur p dictʳ Rege		xiijs.	iiijd.	
Thornhey	vjli	xjs.		
Stow merket	iiijli	xixs.		
haule taxatʳ ad xᵐ·	vijli	viijs.		
Unde p donatʳ p dictʳ Regē		xls.		
Sm̄ hundrᵈ β̄ dict	xliili	vjs	iiijd	q̖
Inde xᵐ̣ᵃ	vijli	viijs.		

hundrᵉ de hoxoñ.

horam cū Alyngtoñ	iiijli	vjs	iiijd.
Unde p donatur p dictʳ Regem		xxvjs.	viijd.
Kelsale cū Carlton		xlvjs.	
Sylham cū Ershām	iiili	xiijs	
Unde p donatur p dictʳ Regm		xxs	
Laxfelde	vli		
Badyngham	vli		xviijd.
Unde p donatur p dictʳ Regem		xs.	
Tatyngstoñ cū Brundyssh		lxxiiijs	iiijd.
denyngtoñ	iiijli		
Unde p donatur p dictʳ Regem		xs	
Wylvey		lviijs.	
Bedyngfeld cū Southoll	iijli	iiijs	ijd
Unde p donatur p dictʳ Regē		xiijs	iiijd.
Stradbroke cum Wyngfeld	ixli		
Unde p donatur p dictʳ Regem		xls.	
Bedfeld cū Saxsted		liijs	iiijd
Unde p donatur p dictʳ Regem		xs.	
Waybred cū Wetherysdale	iiijli	xiijs.	iiijd.
Unde p donatur p dictʳ Regem		xvjs.	
ffresyngfeld cū Wetyngham & Chebenhale hamelette }	viijli	xs	iiijd.
Unde p donatur p dictʳ Regem		ls	
Mendham cum Metfield		vij	ob
Unde p donatur p dictʳ Regem		xxvjs.	viijd.
hoxoñ cū debenham	xjli	viijd	
Unde p donatur p dictʳ Regem		xxxijs.	xd
Wyrlyngworth cum Sohm̄	vli		
Unde p donatur p dictʳ dom̃ Regem		xs	
Sm hundrᵉ β̄ dictʳ ——iijˣˣ	iijli	xvjd	ob

hundred de Blything

Bronfeld cū pesenale et mell	iiijli	xixs	xid
Walpole cū Syptoñ & Cokeley	iiijli	vs.	ixd.
Unde p donatur p dictʳ Regem		xvs	
Upstoñ cū henenynghm̄		xlvijs	xd
Bramstoñ cū Stobene	iiijli		
Unde p donatur p dictʳ Regem		xxvjs	
Medyltoñ cū ffordle		xliijs	vd.

Unde p donatur p dict͞s Regem		viijs.	
Hensted		xxxvjs	id.
huntyngfeld cū lynsted magna & pua	iijli	iijs	iiijd.
Unde p donatur p dict͞s Regem		xxiiijs	
henghm̄		xxviijs.	
Unde p donatur p dict͞s Regem		xs.	
Soterton̄		xxijs	
Unde p donatur p dict͞s Regem		iiijs	
Eston		xxxvjs	viijd
Unde p donatur p dict͞s Regem		viijs.	
Southcoue		xxixs	vid.
Unde p donatur p dict͞s Regem		vjs	
Southwolde	iiili	xiis	iid.
Thornyngton̄ cū Wenaston̄		xlixs.	iiijd.
Unde p donatur p dict͞s Regem		xijs.	
Westhale		liiijs.	
Unde p donatr̄ p dict͞s Regem		xs.	
Chedeston̄ cū Blyford	vli		
Unde p donatur p dict͞s dom̄ Regem		xxs.	
Benacre Bulcamp cū Bregg	vli	vjs.	viijd
Unde p donatur p dict͞s Regem		xijs	
hasylworth	iiijli		iid.
Unde p donatur p dict͞s Regem		xijs	
Onehale cum ffrostendon̄	iijli	xjs	
Unde p donatur p dict͞s Regem		xs	
Blyburgh cū Walberswyke	vjli	xiijs	xd.
Unde p donatur p dict͞s Regem		xvjs	
Wrenhm̄	iijli	viijs.	
Reydon	iijli	iijs	ob q
Westylton̄	vli	vijs	vid.
Unde p donatur p dict͞s Regem		viijs.	
leyston̄ cum Sysewell	viijli		xvjd.
Unde p donatur p dict͞s Regem		xs	
Northalys	ixli		
Unde p donatur p dict͞s Regem		xviijs.	
Cratfeld		lis.	viijd.
Unde p donatur p dictū Regem		xiiijs.	
Dersham cum Yoxford	vli		xijd
Unde p donatur p dict͞s Regem		xviijs.	
Wycett Rumbrugh Speksale & holton̄	vjli		
Unde p donatur p dict͞s Regem		xxxs.	
Sm̄ hundre p dict͞s	⁊ vli	xvs	

hundrᵈ de Waynford

Wyrlynghm̄ cū Cone	iijli	iijs	xd
Unde p donatur p idem Regem		ixs	

Rynglesfeld cū Redeshm̄		xlijs.	vid	
Unde p donatur p dictɔ Regem		xijs.		
Sotyrle cū chadynfeld & Wyllynghm̄	vli	xvjs.		
Unde p donatʳ p dictɔ Regem		xijs.		
Bungey	vjli	vjs	vjd.	
Unde p donatʳ p dictɔ Regē		xxvjs.		
Beclys	xiijli	iiijs	iijd.	
Bersham in Shipmedowe	ijli	xiijs.		
Unde p donatur p dictɔ Regem		xijs.		
metyngham		xlixs	ix.	
Unde p donatur p dictɔ Regem		xs		
Ilketsale	vijli	xiijs	viid	
Unde p donatur p dictɔ Regem		xxvjs.		
Westoñ Elw & Upredeshm̄ } Taxantur ad xᵐ	iiijli	xvs.		
Unde p donatur p dictɔ Regem		xxs.		
Southelmhm̄	xiiijli	xiijs	iiid	ob
Unde p donatur p dictɔ Regē	iiijli			
Sm̄ hundrɔ p dictɔ	lxvli	xixs	viijd	ob
Inde xᵐ	iiijli	xvs.		

hundrɔ de lothynglond

Blundestone		lvs	xjd	
Unde p donatur p dictɔ Rege'		xvjs.		
Olton cum fflyxtoñ		xlvijs.	viijd	ob
Unde p donatur p dictɔ Regē		xs.		
heryngflete		xxxs.		
Unde p donatur p dictɔ Regē		viijs.		
Askeby		xxijs.		
Unde p donatur p dictɔ Regē		viijs.		
Bradwelle		xliijs	iijd	q
lounde		xls	viijdob	q
Unde p donatur p dictɔ Rege		xs.		
Belton	iijli	xiijs	iijd	q
Unde p donatur p dictɔ doᵐ Rege		xiijs	iiijd.	
Burgh		xvs	vijd.	
hoptoñ		xxxiijs	viijd	
ffretoñ		xls.		
Unde p donatur p dictɔ Regem		xijs		
Guntoñ		xxixs.		
Unde p donatur p dictɔ Regem		xijs.		
Corton	iijli		xvjd.	
Unde p donatur p dictɔ Regem		xiijs	iiijd.	
Som̄letoñ		liijs.	viijd.	
Unde p donatur p dictɔ Regem		xs.		
lowystoft taxatʳ ad xᵐ	iijli	xvs	iid	q
Gorlestoñ taxatur ad xᵐ		lvs	xd ob	q

Reystoñ cū Gorlestoñ	vj*li*	iiijs	iiijd.
Unde p donatur p dicts Regē		xxs.	vjd.
pua Jernemuth cū Northmll	iij*li*	xvjs	viijd
Unde p donatur p dicts Regem		xxs.	
Sm̄ hundrꝑ ꝑ dc̄i	xliij*li*	xixs.	ijd.
Inde xᵐ	vj*li*	xjs.	

hundrꝑ de Mutford.

Kessynglond	v*li*	viijs.	vijd
Unde p donatur p dicts Regē		xxs.	
pakefeld cū Kyrkeley	iij*li*		ijd ob
Gyssylham cū pte de Reysshemere	iij*li*	iiijs	iiijd
Unde p donatur p dicts Regem		xiijs	iiijd.
mutford cū Banabye et pte Reysshemere	iij*li*	ijs.	
Unde p donatur p dicts Regē		xiijs	iiijd.
Carleton		liis.	
Unde p donatur p dicts Regē		xs.	
Sm̄ hundrꝑ ꝑ dicts	xvij*li*	vijs	jd ob

ltm xxiiij s ob p mas̄ſys de Cretyng & mekylfeld
que fuer̄ abbie de Grasteno Aliengine
hic Incipit libtas Sā Edmundi
& villa de Bury Sc̄i Edī — xxiiij*li*

hundred de Babbergh.

Stoke	iiij*li*	xvs	vjd.
Cavendessh		ꝗ ixs	viijd. ob
Waldyngfeld magna	iiij*li*	vjs	viijd ob q
Unde de xxᵒ bonoꝝ Augusts le Waleys		xiiijs	iiijd.
Neylond	iij*li*		
Corneherde magna		xlviijs	vjd.
Unde p donatur p dicts Regem		xijs	iiijd.
Corneherde pua		xlis	jd.
Unde p donatur p dicts Regem		xs	iiijd.
Newtoñ		xlvijs	ijd.
Unde p donatur p dicts Regem		xvs	
lausille	iij*li*	xvijs	viijd.
Unde p donatur p dicts Rege		xs.	
Illey combust		lvijs	iijd
Unde p donatur p dicts Regē		viijs	
Bures	iij*li*	iiijs.	
Unde p donatur p dicts Rege		viijs.	
Oerthest		xxxviijs	viijd.
Unde p donatʳ p dicts Regem		iiijs.	
Som̄ton		xxxiijs.	
Unde p donatur p dicts Rege		viijs.	iiijd.
Alfeton		xxiijs.	ixd.
Unde p donatur p dicts Regem			xxjd.

Asyngtoñ	iijli		vd.
Unde p donatur p dicts dom Regem		vijs.	
Syymplyng	iijli	iijs	iijd ob
Unde p donatur p dicts Regem		xs.	
Boxtede		xxxvjs.	
Unde p donatur p dicts Regem		vs.	
Polstede	iijli	iijs	viijd.
Unde p donatur p dicts Regem		viijs.	
Westone		xLiijs	iiijd.
Unde p donatur p dicts Regem		xs	xd.
Prestone		Liijs.	
Unde p donatur p dicts Regem		xviijs	iiijd.
Waldyngfeld pua		Ls.	
Boxford		xLixs	ixd ob
Cokefeld	iiijli	xvs.	
Unde p donatur p dicts Regem		xvjs.	
Unde de xvs bonoȝ Barthi Burgherssh		xxs.	
Aketon	iijli	xiiijs	iid obq
Unde p donatur p dicts Regem		xiijs	iiijd
Groten		xLis	viijd ob
Unde p donatur p dicts Regem		xs	
Stansted		xLiijs	viijd q
Unde p donatur p dicts Regem		vjs	
Illey moñachȝ		Liijs	iiijd ob
Meldyng		Lijs	iiijd ob
Unde p donatur p dicts Regem		xijs.	
Edwardeston	iijli	xiijs.	
lavenham	vijli	vjs	vd.
Glemefford	iijli	xvs	vjd
Melleford	vijli	vis	vd.
Sutbury	xviijli	xiiijs.	
Sm̃ hundrę p̃ dcī	q xixli	xixs	xd ob q

hundrdę de Cofford.

Bylstoñ		Lviijs	ob
Aldham		xviijs	ob
Unde p donatur p dicts dom Regem		xs.	ob
Elmesset		xLvjs.	iiijd.
hegham	vli	viijs	iijd.
Ketelbreston		xxxiiijs	ijd
Unde p donatur p dicts Regem		vijs.	
Kersey		Lvjs	ixd.
Reddyng		xxxiiijs	xd
Unde p donatur p dicts Regē		vijs.	
Chelesworth		xxvjs	ob q
Unde p donatur p dicts Regē			xijd ob q
Watefeld cū Naketoñ	iijli	xiiijs	iijd.

17

Unde p donatur p dict Regē		xiijs	vd.
Gemeré		xxjs	
Unde p donatur p dict Regem		vs.	
lelesheye		xxxvijs	iid.
leyham		xlvs	viijd ob
Unde p donatur p dict Regem		vijs	iijd ob
Thorpmoriens		lvjs.	
Unde p donatur p dict Regem		vjs.	
hadley	viijli	xs	
Bretenhm̄		ls	
Unde p donatur p dict Regem		vjs	
Wathcshm̄		xxxvijs.	iiijd.
Unde p donatur p dict Regem		viijs.	
Sm̄ hundrẹ p̄ dcī	xlvli	iijs	xid ob q

hundred de Theugowe

ffornhm̄ Om̄i Scoʒ		xxxvjs.	
Unde p donatur p dict Regem			xld
Chelmyngton	iiijli	xs.	
Unde p donatur p dict Regem		xxs.	
Ikeworth		xlixs	
Unde p donatur p dict Regem		viijs.	
Brokeleye cum Rede		lviijs	viijd.
Unde p donatur p dict Regem		vijs	
lakford	iijli	xvs	viijd.
Unde p donatur p dict Regem		xiijs.	
Saxhm̄		xxxvjs	iiijd.
Unde p donatur p dict Regem		xjs	xd.
hemgrave		xxviijs	ixd.
Unde p donatur p dict Regem		vs	xid.
hornyngẹ herthe magna		liijs	iiijd.
Unde p donatur p dict Regem		viijs.	
hargūe		lis	viijd.
Unde p donatur p dict Regem		xs	
Kenton		xxxs	iijd ob
Unde p donatur p dict Regem		iiijs	
Saxham pua		ls	ijd.
Unde p donatur p dict Regē		vijs.	
hausted		lvs	viijd.
Unde p donatur p dict Regem		ixs	
Rysby	iijli	xiijs	iijd
Westele		xliiijs.	
Unde p donatur p dict Regem		vjs.	
hornyngẹ herth pua		xixs	jd.
Unde p donatur p dict Regem		iiijs	viijd.
Barwe	iiijli		
Unde p donatur p dict Regem		ixs	

E

fflemptoñ		xxxvijs	ijd.
Unde p donatur p dictᵒ Regem		vjs	xd
Whepsted	iijli		jd
Sm̄ hundrᵉ β dcī	lxvjli	ixs	iijd ob

hundred de Thedwardestrᵉ

Bertoñ		viijli	xis	vd
Unde p donatur p dictᵒ Regē	iijli		
heggessete cū Beketoñ	iiijli	iijs	viijd
Unde p donatur p dictᵒ Regē		iijs	viijd.
levermer magna	iijli	xixs.	vd
Unde p donatur p dictᵒ Regem		vjs.	
Wolpett		xliijs	iiijd
Creukeston	iijli	xvijs	vd.
Unde p donatur p dictᵒ Regem		iiijs	ixd.
Ratlesdeñ		xlixls.sicviijd.	
Roughm̄	iiijli	ijs	iijd.
Unde p donatur p dictᵒ Regem		vijs.	
Tostoke		xls.	
Unde p donatur p dictᵒ Regem		ijs.	
ffornhm̄		xlvjs	vjd
Whelnethm̄ magna & pua		lijs	iiijd ob q
Unde p donatᵗ p dictᵒ Regem		vijs.	iiijd.
Geddyng cū ffelshm̄	iiijli	iijs	iijd ob
Unde p donatur p dictᵒ Regē		xjs.	vd.
Tymworth cū Ampton	iiijli	xjs	iiijd.
Unde p donatur p dictᵒ Regem		vjs	iiijd.
Thurstoñ		lvijs	viijd
Unde p donatur p dictᵒ Regem		ijs	viiid
Stanfeld cum Bradle pua	iiijli		
Unde p donatur p dictᵒ Regem		vijs	xd.
pakenhm̄	vli	xiijs.	vjd.
Unde p donatur p dictᵒ Regem		ixs.	vjd.
Bradefeld monachoʒ		xlvs.	
Unde p donatur p dictᵒ Regem		vs	vijd.
Bradfeld Seyntkelerᵉ		xxijs.	
Unde p donatur p dictᵒ Regem		ijs.	
Rosshbrook		xxvijs	iiijd.
Unde p donatur p dictᵒ Regem		vs	vjd.
Sm̄ hundrᵉ β dcī	lxijli	vijs	ijd ob

hundrᵉ de Blakeborune.

Ixeworthe		xlvs	iiijd.
Unde p donatur p dictᵒ Regem		vjs	viijd.
hopton	iiijli	iijs	vjd.
heldercle		xxxiijs.	
Unde p donatur p dictᵒ Regem		vijs	iijd.

ffakenham pua		xxxixs.	
Unde p donatur p dicto Regem		vijs.	
Stantoñ	iijli	xvjs	viijd
leūmere pua		liis	vd.
Unde p donatur p dicto Regem		xjs.	
Eustone		liijs.	
Inghm̄		xlvs.	
Unde p donatur p dicto Regem		ixs	ixd.
Weston		liiijs	
Unde p donatur p dicto Regem		xiijs	iiijd.
Berhm̄	iijli	vjs.	
Aysshefeld magna		xlijs.	
hepworthe	iiijli	iijs	iiijd.
Rokynghale		xlviijs	jd.
Elineswell		liijs	vjd.
Nortoñ	iijli	vs	iiijd.
Berdewelle	vijli		ijd.
Aysshefelde pua		liijs	iiijd.
Unde p donatur p dicto Regem			xld.
Coneweston̄	iijli	ix	vjd.
Capstoñ		xls	viijd.
Bernynghm̄	iijli	xijs	xjd.
Reyssheworth		xvjs	
Enateshale		liijs.	
Unde p donatur p dicto Regem		iijs	ixd.
Troston̄	iijli	viijs	iiijd.
ffakenhm̄ magna		xlijs	vjd.
laughm̄		xxxjs.	
Telvehm̄		xliiijs	xjd.
Stowelangtofte		xxxvjs	xd ob
hunteston̄		xxxvjs.	
Ixworth thorpe		xxxvjs	iiijd.
honeweton		liijs	vjd.
Watleffeld		liijs	vjd.
Walshm̄		lvjs	viijd.
Westowe	iijli		
Wrydewelle		xlijs	vjd.
Unde p donatur p dicto Regem		xs	iijd.
Culford		xxxiiijs	viijd.
Unde p donatur p dicto Regem		xiijs.	
Sm̄ hundrẹ ꝑ dcī iiij^{xx}	xvli	xvs	iijd ob

hundrẹ de lakford.

Mildenhale	xjli	xs	jd ob q
Brandon		xvijs	iiijd.
Iklynghm̄	vjli	ijs	viijd.
Unde p donatur p dicto dom Regem		ijs	vijd.

lakynghethe	vj*li*	xixs	ixd q
Unde p donatur p dicts Regem		xviijs.	
heryngeswelle	iii*li*	xiiijs.	
Unde p donatur p dicts Regem		xijs	vijd
Eryswelle	vij*li*		ixd.
Unde p donatur p dicts Regem		xxijs.	vjd.
Eluedene	iiij*li*		
heghm̄		xljs	iijd ob q
Unde p donatur p dicts Regem			xvd ob
Dounham		liijs	iiijd.
Unde p donatur p dicts Regem		xs	vjd.
Cavenhm̄	iij*li*	iijs.	
Unde p donatur p dicts Regē		xijs	iiijd.
Wrydlyngtoñ	v*li*	xs.	
Unde p donatur p dicts Regē		xxs.	
ffrekenhm̄	iiij*li*	xiiijs	iiijd ob
Unde p donatur p dicts Regē		ixs.	
Wangford		lvjs	vd.
Unde p donatur p dicts Regē			xvijd.
Tudenhm̄	iiij*li*	iijs	jd q
Unde p donat' p dicts Regem		xvs.	
Bertoñ pua	ij*li*	xs	iiijd.
Unde p donat p dicts Regem		xs	vjd.
Sm̄ hundre de p dci	lxxiij*li*	xvjs	vjd ob

hundre de Ryssebregge.

Denhm̄		xlvs	vd.
Unde p donat' p dicts Regem		viijs.	
haūhill	vj*li*	xvs	viijd ob
Kedyton	iij*li*	viijs	viijd.
Depdeñ cū Cheldebergh	iij*li*	xiijs	iiijd.
Unde p donatur p dicts dōm Regē		xiiijs	vjd.
Bradley pua		xxxs.	
Unde p donatur p dicts Regem		vijs.	
honedoñ	iiij*li*		xxiijd ob
Unde p donatur p dicts Regem		vijs	viiijd.
Unesdene		xxxijs	iiijd.
Bernerdestoñ		xliijs.	
Thirlowe magna		lviijs	iiijd q
Wykhm̄ Broke	viij*li*	iijs	iiijd
Unde p donatur p dicts Regē		xxs.	
Stradeshyll cū denarestoñ	iij*li*	xiijs.	
Unde p donatur p dicts Regē		vjs	viijd.
hakedone cū Thurstantoñ		xlijs	iiijd.
Unde p donatur p dicts Regem		ixs.	
Clare	v*li*		
Wrotyng magna	iij*li*		vd

Stanefeld		xliis	iiijd
Wydekeshoo		xxixs	ixd
Unde p donatur p dicts Regem		viijs.	
Multoñ	iiijli	vjs	viiid
pollyngworth cū Chopeley		liijs	ijd.
Unde p donatur p dicts Regem		vijs.	
Thirlowe pua		lvs	iiijd ob
Dalham cū Tunstall		lvijs	iiijd.
Stoke Chiltoñ and Boyton	vli	iis	ixd ob q
Unde p donatur p dicts Rege		xviijs.	
Wrotyng pua	iijli	iijs	xd.
Unde p donatur p dicts dom Regem		vjs.	
Bradley magna	iijli	xs	xid ob
Wetheresfelde	iijli	vjs	ob q
lydgate	vli		xvd
Unde p donatur p dicts Regem		viijs	
Gayslee cū Nedhm et kenford	vli	iijs	iiijd.
Coulyng	iijli	xiiijs	q
Unde p donatur p dicts Regem		xs	
Sm hundre p dci iijxx	xviijli	xvs	vd ob
Ixnyng di hundre	xiiijli	iiijs	ijd
Unde p donatur p dictū Rege		xs.	
Bona mobilia Johis Tendryng invents in villa de Stokenaylond polsted and Sprowtoñ ad xvm p se ad Summam		xxs	ixd.
Sm di hundre cū bonis mobilibz	xvli	iijs	xid.
Sm To.te libtatis Sci Edmundi cū di hundre de Ixnyng & bonis mobilibz Johis Tendryng	Smiij li xx	xiis	ob q

hic incipit libtas Scē Etheldrede

hundre de plomesgate

Benhale Saxmūdhm and ffarmhm	iiijli	xiiijs	vd.
Unde p donatur p dicts Rege		xxs	vjd.
Aldeburgh cū haswode		lvjs	viijd.
Unde p donatur p dicts Regem		xs.	
Ikne cum Chesylford and Onynglborth		xlvijs.	
Unde p donatur p dicts Regem		vjs	
Sternefeld		xxxvjs	ijd.
Unde p donatur p dicts Rege		viijs	
Glemhm pua cū Stratford		xlvijs	
Unde p donatur p dicts Rege		xiijs	iiijd
Glemhm magna		xliijs.	
Unde p donatur p dicts Regē		iijs.	
Sudburne		liiijs	
Unde p donatur p dicts Regem		xxs.	

Rendhm̄ cum Brosyerd	iiijli	iiijs	xd.
Unde p donatur p dictṣ Regē		xiijs	
Blaxhale cū pte de Tunstall		liiijs	xd.
Unde p donatur p dictṣ Regem		vjs	
Snape cū ffrestoñ		liiijs.	
Unde p donatur p dictṣ Regem		xiijs	iiijd.
Cranyfford cū Swystlyng	iijli	xis	vd.
Unde p donatur p dictṣ Rege		viijs.	
Perhm̄		xliiijs	
Unde p donatur p dictṣ Rege		xs.	
Wanysden cum pte de Tunstall		lijs	ixd
Sm̄ hundrẹ p̄ dcī	xxxvijli		xiijd.

hundrẹ de Wylford

Aldertoñ		liiijs.	viijd
Unde p donatur p dictṣ Regem		xs	
Baudesey	vijli		xijd.
Unde p donatur p dictṣ Regem		xxxiijs	iiijd.
Sutton	iijli	vjs	viijd.
Unde p donatur p dictṣ Regem		vs.	
Boyton cum Capell		xxxvijs	vjd.
Unde p donatur p dictṣ Regem		viijs.	
Rameshalt cū Bromeswell		xls.	
Unde p donat' p dictṣ Regem		vs	
hollysle cū Chatyshm̄		xliijs	iiijd.
Unde p donatur p dictṣ Regem		xxs	
Wykhm̄ cū petryste and loudhm̄	iijli	xis	iijd.
Unde p donatur p dictṣ Regem		xs.	
Boulge debache and Dalanghoo		xliiijs	iiijd
melton cū Ufford	iiijli	iijs	iiijd.
Unde p donatur p dictṣ Regem		viijs.	
Bredfeld taxatur ad xam		xvjs	vd
Sm̄ hundrẹ p̄ dcī	xxviijli	xixs	vjd.
Inde xmạ		xvjs	vd.

hundrẹ de lose

hachestoñ		xlvjs.	
letherynghm̄ cū Chasfeld	iijli	iiijs	vjd.
Unde p donatur p dictṣ Regē		xijs	
Estoñ cū Ketelbregh		lijs	vjd
Unde p donatur p dictṣ Regem		vjs.	
Unde de xma de bonis Augustṣ waleys		xs	vijd.
Cretynghm̄ cū Brandestoñ and Monewedene	₵	xjs	viijd.
Unde p donatur p dictṣ Rege		viijs	
Aysshe		xlis	
Rendeleshm̄	iijli	viijs	viijd.
Unde p donatur p dictṣ Regem		xs	

Sohm cū Kenton	iijli	vijs	
Unde p donatur p dicts Regē		xijs	
fframlynghm	iijli	xiijs	iiijd
Unde p donatur p dicts Regē		xs.	
Eyke		xLvjs	viijd.
Unde p donatur p dicts Regē		xxs	
hoo dalanghoo & Wodbregg	iiijli	xxs	xd
Unde p donatur p dicts Regem		xijs	
Marlesford cū pte de Butle		xLvijs	
Unde p donatur p dicts Regē		xs	vjd.
Sm hundrf þ dcī	xxxvli	xiiijs	vijd

hundrf de Carleford.

Wytleshm	iijli	vijs	iiijd.
Ryssehmere cū Alesborne		xLiiijs	ixd
Unde p donatur p dicts Regē		xviijs	xd ob
Playford cū Brightwell		Lvijs.	
Unde p donatur p dicts Regē		xs.	
Todynhm cū Culpho	iijli		
Unde p donatur p dicts Regē		ixs	
Grondesburgh cū burgh	iijli	xvijs	q
Unde p donatur p dicts Regē		xs	
Belyngf magna & pua	iiijli	vjs	
Unde p donatur p dicts Regē		xs	
hakeston		Lvjs	
Unde p donatur p dicts Regē		xijs.	
Clopton	iiijli	vs.	
Unde p donatur p dicts Regem		xiijs	iiijd.
Martleshm		Lviijs.	
Unde p donatur p dicts Regem		xs.	
ffoxhole cū Kesgraue		xxxjs	vjd.
Unde p donatur p dicts Regē		xijs	
Otleigh	iijli		xd.
Sm hundrf þ dcī	xxxvli	iijs	vd ob

hundrf de Coleneyse.

Tremley and Tremley cum Altestoñ	vijli	vjs	xd.
Unde p donatr p dicts Regem		xxxiijs.	iiijd.
Naketon leuyngtoñ & Strattoñ	iijli	xijs.	
Unde p donatur p dicts Regem		xiij	iiijd.
Kyrketoñ ffaltenhm Bucleshm & Olmeslee	vijli	vjs.	
Unde p donatur p dicts Regem		xLs	
Waltoñ & ffylchestowe	vjli	iijs	viijd.
Unde p donatur p dicts Regem		xxxiijs	iiijd.
Sm hundrf þ dcī	xxiiijli	xs	vjd.

hundrₑ de Thredlyng

Assheffeld cum Thorp		xlvjs	iiijd.
Unde p donatur p dictₚ Regem		vjs	viijd
fframesden cum Pethaugh		xliijs	iiijd.
Debynhm̄ cum Wyston	vli	xs	ijd.
Unde p donatur p dictₚ Regem		xiis	ijd.
Sm̄ hundrₑ β dcl		xli	xd
Sm̄ toᵗ libtatₑ ⎫ Soč Etheldrede ⎭	iiijˣˣ xlli	xs	ixd ob

I am not acquainted with a perfect book of taxation belonging to any one county of so early a date as the foregoing. In the Chetham Library at Manchester, there is a complete list of taxes for the County of Lancaster, but this goes no further back than the middle of the 17th Century.

It may reasonably be supposed that the principle which guided our ancestors in the making of this early assessment, was akin to that which we now term 'rateable value.' We find at a later period (4 Henry VIII. A.D. 1513) that, for the "raysing of a whole taxe granted to the King," the different parishes in the Town of Ipswich were assessed as follows:—

St. Mary le Tower	£5	4	0	St. Mary Elms	£2 18 0
St. Margaret	5	11	0	St. Lawrence	5 5 6
St. Clement	4	9	8	St. Mary at the Quay	4 9 4
St. Nicholas	2	4	0	St. Peter	4 6 4
St. Stephen	2	4	8	St. Matthew	4 3 0

St. Helen 13s. 4d.

the total sum of which is a few shillings in excess of the actual sum at which the Burgesses of the Town were assessed in the Taxation of Henry VI. For the levying of this later Ipswich tax, two Taxers and two Collectors were nominated for each parish.

The Suffolk Taxation list gives as good an idea of the position held by the several parishes and townships in the early part of the 15th Century as could well be desired. It is interesting to note the change that has passed over many of these places since the time when the assessment was made. To give a solitary instance, drawn almost at random from the Hundred of Lothingland: the villages of Belton and Corton are each taxed at only a few shillings less than the adjacent town of Lowestoft, which itself could then have been little more than a fishing village.

The names of places as formerly written, additions made thereto, and the mention of places no longer to be found recorded in lists of Suffolk parishes, *etc.*, are in many cases well worth notice.

A tax imposed on every parish in the Kingdom, in the year 1370, was at a *uniform* rate, the larger in each Hundred being commanded to help the smaller.

This account of the Taxes payable by the county of Suffolk, is followed by a curious heraldic description of the arms borne by divers Sovereigns, with the designation of the several supporters placed at the head of each. (*temp.* Henry VI.) It was possibly deemed absolutely necessary that an important maritime town like Ipswich should possess an authoritative document of this kind, but it is a reasonable supposition that it was not very frequently referred to.

"THE MOST CRISTEN KYNG OF FFRAUNCE* his grace berith Assure thre flowre delice golde Garuntyn

THE MOSTE EXCELLENT & MOST REDOUBTED KYNG OF ENGLOND† my most Soﬀraigne lorde berith quartly Asure iij. ﬄoure delice golde and he berith Gowlys thre lypardys‡ passaunts golde enarmed in asure.

ANTYLOPE

THE KYNG OF SPAYNE. his noble grace berith quartly Gowlys. A castell golde And he berith Syluer A lyon Salijaunt Sable.

TYGYR

THE KYNG OF POYLE.§ he berith gowlys departed wt. a Crosse golde.

---

* This was the ordinary title of the Kings of France: it is ancient, but of uncertain origin.
† This title is not older than the latter part of the 14th Century.
‡ *Leos-pardes*, not leopards. Until late in the 14th Century, the lions of the Royal Shield of England were known as leopards. It was an heraldic title only, denoting the precise attitude of the lion, walking and looking about him after the manner of a leopard.
§ Poland.

An Egle Syluer And he berith gowlys a Kyng coraious syttyng crownyd and armyd in gold sittyng uppoñ a cowrser off syluer Rynnyng empailed in ūto.

BOUAS:

THE KYNG OF AROGOWEÑ* he berith golde iiij palys gowlis.

DAMA:

THE KYNG OF DENMARKE he berith quarterly golde hartele gowlys iij. lypardes passaunte assure. And he berith gowlys a lyoñ of golde seaunt in a cheire of Syluer wepenyd wᵗ the same.

HERTE.

THE KYNG OF HOUGARY. he berith quarterly asure thre Sunnys golde and he berith gowlys A syluer ffecy of vj:

IBEX

THE KYNG OF CYPRESSE he berith quarterly sylū and asure ffecy a lyon Rampaunt gowlys And he berith syluer a crosse potaney golde betwē iiij of the same.

GEROSYLL.

THE KYNG OF BEAME.† he berith gowlys a lyone. Rampaunt Rewardyng fforce syluer crowned and armyd in golde.

GENEROWNYS.

THE KYNG OF NAPLYS he berith quarterly veert. ij. lyons passaunte golde. And he berith gowlys a Crosse matale golde

PARAUNDYR

THE KYNG OF CECYLE. he bereth golde iij. pales. gowles. ij. voydures poynted syluer wᵗ ij. Eglys displayed Cubyll membrye with gowlys.

GRYFFOWN.

THE KYNG OF GRYCE. he berith a crosse fuse Crosse gowlys in a Champe of golde upoñ a felde of verte.

PANTER

THE KYNG OF NAVERNE.‡ he berith quarterly assure. iij flowre delyce golde wᵗ a bende gobony gowlys & syluer And he berith gowlys A charbokyll gold.

BRADRIX.

THE KYNG OF PORTYUGALE. he berith v. skochones eneroys asure ītele psaut wᵗ a bordure gowlys castell golde.

* Arragon, the eastern part of Spain † Bohemia ‡ Navarre.

UNYCORNE.

THE KYNGE OF SKOTTYS. he berith golde a lyoñ Rampaunt w⁺ in a doble trussure count fforete gowlys

OLYFAUNT."

There is every reason to suppose that this description as it stands is unique: it is certainly of great interest.

The list of Knights' Fees of the Honors of Lancaster and Leicester, lying within the County of Suffolk, also finds a place in the Little Domesday Book.* Several such lists, and especially those annexed to the Duchies of Lancaster and Leicester, from various counties, are to be found in many of our public libraries, but Sims, who gives a lengthy account of these Knights' Fees in his "Manual," makes no mention of those old hereditary revenues here given, and which may be supposed to be generally unknown to students.

"HEC SUNT FEODA MILITUM DE HONORIBUS LANECASTR' ET LEYCEST' IN COMUTAT' SUFF:

In villa de Lund cum membris	j. feod militis
In villa de Ilkttleshale cū membris	ij. feod & dī milit
In villa de Mendhm̄ cū membris	j. feod militis
In villa de Wytynhm̄ cū membris	j. feod militis
In villa de Akenhm̄ cū membris	j. feod militis
In villa de Hasketoñ clopton. & Wodebregge cū membris	j. feod militis
In villa de Ikene cū membris	j. feod militis
In villa de Oteleye cū membris	j. feod & dī militis
In villa de Cleydone cū membrę	Dī feod militis
In villa de Culfo cum membrę	Dī feod militis
In halghetre & Alnesburne cū membrę	tres ptes viiiᵒ feod
In lellesseye cū membris	Dī feod militis
In Sproutoñ cū membris	iij feod militis
In Wylasham cū membris	j feod militis

* Add MS 25,012 fol. 47 b. Br: Mus.

In Offtone cū membris	- -	*j feod militis*
In pua Blakenhm̄ cū membris	- -	*qrt feod militis*
In Ryseby cū membris	- -	*j feod militis*
In ffyneberghe cū membris	- -	*ij feod militis*
Buxhale cum membris		*j feod militis*
In Thorp moriens cū membrę	- -	*ij feod militis*
In prestone cū membrę	- -	*Dī feod militis*
In Waldingfelde cū membrę	- -	*Dī feod militis*
In Boxtede cum membrę	- -	*Dī feod militis*
In Thurstantoñ cū membę	- -	*j feod militis*
In Baudreseye cū membrę	- -	*ij feod militis*
In veteri Newton cū membrę		*vij ps viiiɈ feod milits*
In Stonhm̄ Count cū membɈ		*xx ps jɈ feod militis*
In leyhm̄ cum membr'	- -	*viij feod militis*

Sm̄ Toᵗ ffeod militū } *xxviij Dī & xxvij ptes*"

In the brief, but singular "Memorandum" of ancient lineal measurements which follows, several points are touched, likely to enlighten us somewhat with regard to a matter which in the state of our present knowledge, is one of the greatest doubt and obscurity, viz., the true value and meaning of the terms anciently employed in such measurements.

"MEMORANDŪ that iiij. Barly cornys takyn̄ in the myddys of the yere (*ear*) makith an unche And xij. unches makith a ffoote iij. foote makith a yerd & xvj. ffoote and a halfe makith a perche & iiij. perches in brede and XL in leynght makith an Akir Lond & iiij acres maketh a yerd of Lond And v yerds makyth a hyde of Londe & viij hydes of Londe & viij hydes of londe makith an Knyght's ffee."

We are at once brought face to face with the familiar fact that the standard of measurement, like that of weight, had its origin in the grain of corn, which was to be "taken in the myddys of the ear." It will be noticed that the number of grains, which according to this note were necessary to complete an inch, were four, whereas it is now but three. The table proceeds pretty much according to our recognised rule as far as the statement that "iiij perches in brede & XL in length makith an aker," then we meet with a "*yerd*," a "*hide*," and a "*Knights' fee*," concerning which there seem to have been no general agreement as to limit or extent. The old *Virgate* or *yerd* (*Sax:* a certain extent of land) is mostly regarded as an indefinite term containing somewhere from 25 to 40 acres, and as a necessary consequence the terms that follow are equally vague. The above "memorandum" which cannot have been framed later than the 15th Century, and probably much earlier, seems to settle the measurements with a certainty which is now scarcely recognised. The "yerd" which is usually accounted only the *fourth* part of a hide, is here reckoned a *fifth*. The "hide" or "caracute," = 120 acres, is a very ancient measurement, having been employed by the Romans: this was apparently the unit of assessment. It doubtless had its origin in the quantity of land that could be enclosed within an Ox hide, when cut into slips and carried round the land so enclosed, although this application of the term is sometimes disputed. It is sometimes called a "plough land"=caracute, owing to the quantity of land being just as much as one plough was capable of cultivating. There is considerable difference of opinion respecting what is known as "a Knights' Fee."* In the old feudal system, every holder of an extent of land called "a knight's fee," was obliged at the instigation either of the king or a superior to whom he owed service, to render according to his tenure, as occasion, and the will of his lord required. The land comprised in such a "fee" was doubtless amply sufficient to allow of a proper discharge of the knightly office, although it is difficult to say precisely what it represented. The general impression seems to be against fixing any certain amount, and it is roughly estimated at from 100 to 500 acres of arable land, but then of course the exact limit to an acre is, as

H

we have seen, somewhat doubtful. It *may* be, that the knights' fee varied in different districts, according to the nature of the soil and other considerations, but this is not very likely; at all events eight hides, (whatever they may have contained) according to the memorandum referred to, went to a Knights' fee. It appears extremely probable that the entry was made in the Ipswich Town Books for the very purpose of settling the difficulties occasioned by so arbitrary an arrangement, but I have not met with a single author acquainted with such a table.

The last portion of this book is occupied by a Rhyming Chronicle of the Kings of England, from William I. to Henry VI., which is of special interest. Little more than a mere surmise led me some time ago to ascribe the authorship of these verses to John Lydgate, the Monk-Poet of Bury Saint Edmunds, and there is every reason to regard this as a probable conjecture. Besides it appears that the lines occur in several old MSS. with some slight variations and additions, and are commonly attributed to Lydgate. There is a copy among the Harleian MSS. in the British Museum (2251. f. 2. b.) with an additional stanza relating to the reign of Edward IV. There is one in the handwriting of Shirley, the transcriber of Chaucer, in the Ashmolean Library (No. 59) at Oxford, and written probably about the year 1456, with additions by other hands. The lines were printed in 1530 by Wynkyn de Worde, with additions to the reign of Henry VIII. The verses also occur in a 15th Century MS. known as the "Historical Collections of a London Citizen," fol. 110—112, with this heading, "Cronycles of alle Kyngys of Englonde aftyr the Conqueste as of thyr namys ande where that they bene i-byryede." This was printed by the Camden Society in 1876, and the additional stanza is inserted from the Harleian MS. There are several variations, the most important of which I have indicated in foot notes to the Ipswich Great Domesday text, which stands altogether unencumbered with notes.

"Willm the Conquero^r

This mighty Willm of Normandy
As Bokys olde makith mencoñ
Be iuste tytle & by his Chevalry
made Kyng by conquest of brutesalbioñ*
putte ought harald and toke possesyoñ
Bare his Crowne full xxj. yere
Buryd at Cane thus seithe the cronyclere

Willms Ruffus

Next in ordrelye Successyon
Willm Ruffus his sone crownyd kynge
whiche to godwarde had noñ deuocioñ
Distroyed Chirches of new & old byldynge
To make a fforest plesaunt for huntynge
xiij yere bare his Crowne in dede
Buryed at Wynchestyr ye may rede.

Henricus Primus

his Brother next callid Harry the ffyrst
was at londoñ crownyd as I fynde
whos Brother Robard Duke of Normandy
gav Warre† the cronycle makith mynde
Reconsiled all ranker sett behynde
ffull xxxj‡ yere be record of wrytynge
he Reignyd And buried att Redyng.

Stephanus.

his brother§ Stevyñ wheñ Herry the first was dede
Toward yngland gaue Crosse his sayle
the Archebysshoppe dyd sett up oñ his hede
A Rich Crowne beyng of councelle.
xix. yers w^t sorowe and grett travayle
bare his crowne & nevyr had Rest
And at ffeūsham lyeth buried in a Chest

---

* in margin, *id est* Englonde   † Ganne hym werry   ‡ xxxiij   § cosyn

Henricus ij⁹

Henry the ij^de soñ of the Impasse.
was crownyd next a full manly knyght
As books of olde pleynly dothe expresse
this seid henry by ffroward force and myght.*
yerys xxxv regnyd as it is made of mynd
Att ffount Everard lyeth buried As I ffynd.

Ricardus p̄mus

Richard his soñ by Successyon.
ffirst of that name stronge hardy & notabyll
was crownyd Kynge callid cure de lyon.
w^t sarasyn̄s heds servyd at his Tabyll
Slayne at Calyas by dethe lamentabyll
the space regnyd fully x† yere
his harte buried at Roone und^r the hie awter.

Iohannes

Nexte Kyng Richard regnyd his brother John
after sone entery in to ffraunce.
lost all Aungee & Normandy A noñ
This Lond enterdicted by his‡ goūnannce.
And as it is putt in remembraunce
xviij yere Kynge of Regioñ§
lyeth at worsettyr deyde of poysoñ.

Henricus iij⁹

Herry the iij^de Soñ of ix yere Age
was at Glowcett^r crownyd as I rede
longe warre he had w^t his baronage
Gretly delicted in Almesse dede
lvj^te yere he regnyd here in dede
buried at Westmyster by recorde of writyng
the day of Seynt Edmūde martir & kyng.‖

---

* This stanza in the Ipswich Domesday MS. has but six lines. In the MS. copy from which the Camden Society printed, the fifth line stands as 'Slowe Thomas (*Bekett* is interlined here in a later hand) for Hooly Chyrche ryght.' The omission from this later MS. is easily understood.

† ix   ‡ mys   § this regyon

‖ Seynt *Edwardi* martir *mayde* & Kyng.

Edwardus p̄mus

Edward the first w⁺ his shanks longe
Was aftir crownyd that was a good knyght.
Wanne Skotlande mager the Skotts stronge
And all Walys in the dispyte of ther myght.
duryng his liff mayntenyd trew & Right
xxxv yere he was here Kyng.
lyeth at Westmynster this is no leasyng.

Edwardus ijᵒ

Edwarde his son callid Carnervan̄
succedyng aftyr to make his Alyaunce
As the Cronycle well reherse can̄
Weddyd the doughter of Kyng of ffraunce
Unto Thom̄s of lancastar he toke venisaunce
xix yeres held here Regaly
Buried at Glowcettᵣ books speciffye.

Edwardus iiiᵒ

Edwarde the iij^{de} borne at Wyndsoore
Whiche in Knyghthood had so great a p̄ce
Enherytour of ffrannce w⁺outen̄ moore
bare in his armys quarto iij fflowre delyce*
And gate Calice hi his prudent device
Regnyd in Inglond lj† yere
lyeth at Westmynster thus saieth the cronycler

Ricūs ijᵒ

The son̄ of p̄nce Edward Richard the ij^{de}
In whos tyme was peaese & great plente.
Weddyd quene Anne of Bowan̄‡ as it is ffounde
Isbell after of ffrannce who lyfte to se.§
xxij. yere he reynyd here p̄de
at Langley buried ffirst so stond the case
After to Westmyster his body caried was.

* quarto *the* fflowre delyce   † lij   ‡ *dele* of Bowan
§ Isbell after of ffrance he lystede to see

Henricus iiij.

Henry the iiij^{te} next crowned in certeyn
A ffamows knyght of grete cemlynesse*
ffrom his exile when he come home ageyn
w^t werre travayled and w^t greate sekenesse
xiiij yers he reigned in sothnesse
lyeth att cawntabury in that holy place
god of his marcy do his sowle grace.

Henricus quītus.

The† fyrst henry of knyghthode lodsterre
Wyse‡ manly pleynly to detmyne.
ffortunate p̄vyd in pease & in werre
grettly exspert in marcy full disciplyne
able to stonde amonge the worthyes is.§
Reigned x yers who that lyst to regarde‖
lyeth at Westmynster by Seynt Edwarde.¶

Henricus Sextus

Henry the Syxte brought forth in** vertu
by Iust tytle and by Inheritannce.
provydyd be forne by the grace of Ihū††
To be crownyd yn Inglond & in ffrannce.‡‡
Reignyned xxxix yere & God gaffe hym sufficiance§§
of v̄tuos lyffe & chose hym for his Knyght
At Wyndesore buried And myracles doth by Goddys myght.‖‖

The abrupt ending of the verses in this Ipswich MS. is significant, and may probably throw some light upon the time of Lydgate's death, which has long been a disputed point. Warton, *(History of English Poetry*, Sec.

---

* semblesse   † v   ‡ wyse *and* manly
§ spousyde the doughter of Fraunce, Katerynne
‖ who lyste to have rewarde   ¶ not far fro Synt Edwarde
** in *alle* vertu
†† provydyd *a* forne by the grace of Ihū Chryste
‡‡ To were ij crownys in Englonde and in Fraunce
§§ To whom God hath gevyn souerayne suffycyaunce
‖‖ Long he hathe rejoysed both by day and nyght.

xxi, Note) thinks that the stanza relating to Edward IV. in the Harleian copy, could scarcely have been written by Lydgate, and gives substantial reasons for his opinion. The fifteenth and last stanza relating to Henry VI., as given in the MSS. of the 'London Citizen,' and that of the Ipswich Domesday volume, differ in this important particular, that, while the one assumes the King to be living, the other distinctly alludes to his burial. It is not unlikely that both versions are correct, and each the work of Lydgate, written at two different periods. It is well to point out the discrepancy which exists between the title as given in the former, and the concluding stanza, which omits the place of burial. I will briefly state my reasons for the conclusion at which I have arrived. The Ipswich Domesday copy, as it now exists in the volume which I have already described, was certainly inscribed there in A.D. 1520, and most likely, as was the case with much other matter forming the same volume, copied from an older MS., that had for some time been deposited among the Town Archives, perhaps even from the time when it was originally written. Especially considering the proximity of the Abbey where Lydgate was an inmate, to the Town of Ipswich, there is strong probability for supposing that this epitomized English history, mellowed into verse, would early find its way into safe custody at Ipswich, and escape receiving additional stanzas of the subsequent reigns of Edward IV, Edward V, Richard III, and Henry VII. Lydgate's memory and genius, if there were no other cause likely to operate in favour of the poem retaining its original features, would probably be sufficient to deter men in the attempt to make any additions.

The remaining portions of this Sixth book are certainly of the time of Henry VI. I am strongly of opinion that the whole of the contents are of the same period, and that the heading 'Edwardus quartus' following Stanza xv, marks the precise time when the work came forth (not necessarily for the first time) from Lydgate's pen, *viz.*, soon after the accession of Edward IV. (cir. 1462), which probably marks the time of Lydgate's decease. He certainly lived until the end of the reign of Henry VI., and nothing is more likely, that in closing this Sovereign's reign, the writer should add the name of the King's successor, who had but lately ascended the throne. Such I am inclined to think is a true account of the authenticity of these verses, drawn from inferences which I cannot but regard as fair and reasonable.

It only now remains to give the stanza which appears in the Harleian copy; it has a very different 'ring' about it to the preceding verses, ascribed to Lydgate, and to my mind plainly points to an author other than he.

"*Edwardus Quartus.*
Comforth all thirsty and drynke with gladness,
Rejoyse with myrth though ye have not to spende,
The tyme is come to avoyden your distres.
Edward the Fourth the old wronges to amend,
Is wele disposed in will; and to defend
His lond and peple indede with kynne and myght
Goode lyf and longe, I pray to God hym send
And that Seynt George be with hym in his hyght."

The object of placing in a collection of this description such apparently extraneous matters as these which occupy the Sixth book, is not quite clear, although certainly they would, as I have shewn, have their use. It may have been out of mere caprice, or for want of a more suitable repository, that they are here entered; certainly it has been the means of preserving to us much interesting matter, which may prove exceedingly useful from other than an antiquarian standpoint, and perchance, when its true value is understood, we shall confess that we can ill afford to spare.

Printed by Libri Plureos GmbH in Hamburg,
Germany